A souvenir guide

Uppark House and Garden
West Sussex

Rebecca Wallis

National Trust

The Significance of Uppark

The traditional spelling 'Up Park' perfectly describes the prime setting of the house and gardens, crowning the South Downs ridge in West Sussex. Uppark is a fine example of a family home built during the golden age of country-house construction in the 17th century, cherished by generations of families and the survivor of turbulent events.

The house was built for Ford, Lord Grey, 1st Earl of Tankerville, c.1690 but the interiors and gardens are predominantly associated with the Fetherstonhaugh family who bought the estate in 1747. Sir Matthew and Sarah, Lady Fetherstonhaugh filled it with British decorative art and extensive sets of paintings acquired on an extended Grand Tour. Later their son, Sir Harry, employed the architect and landscape designer Humphry Repton to make changes to the approach, gardens and interiors. Sir Harry's wife Mary Ann and her sister Frances steered Uppark through the 19th century, handing it over to the Meade-Fetherstonhaugh family who undertook much-needed conservation in the 1930s and 40s, yet still preserving its late 18th- and early 19th-century character.

This undisturbed nature of Uppark is one of the elements that make it so important, together with the sheer beauty of the ensembles and the outstanding setting. The house, its principal contents and immediate land came to the National Trust in 1954. A devastating fire in 1989 gutted many of the interiors but they were painstakingly reconstructed and the house reopened in 1995. Uppark today is presented as it was on the day before the fire in 1989 and work continues to show the house and gardens as created by the Fetherstonhaugh family.

Opposite The south front, which looks out over the South Downs

The People of Uppark

This prominent section of the South Downs ridge has drawn people since early human history. Archaeology has revealed Neolithic and Bronze Age (c.4,000–700 BC) objects in the surrounding area along with evidence of later Iron Age and Roman settlements (c.800 BC–AD 410).

In the Anglo-Saxon period the 'manor' of Harting, in which Uppark now sits, belonged to Countess Gytha, wife of Earl Godwine and mother to King Harold. The land subsequently formed part of estates belonging to Robert de Montgomery (d.1094), given to him by the conquering William I (c.1028–87) in exchange for his services at the Battle of Hastings (1066).

Robert's descendant, William d'Aubigny, 1st Earl of Arundel (c.1109–76) granted the land as a 'Knight's fee' to the Hussey family in the mid-12th century, and by 1266 permission had been granted by Henry III to 'fortify and crenelate' a residence 'wherever they please in the manor of Harting'. This was probably near to the present church in Harting, and from 14th-century descriptions of Harting Place it included several gardens, a prison and two enclosed parks; le Netherpark to the north and le Overpark to the south. The southern park became known as le Upparke (later Uppark) and was stocked with deer from c.1332. Two-thirds of the land, cleared of trees, was given over to pasture for grazing animals. By 1440 both parks were leased to Robert Legge, a London draper, and the next owner, Edmund Ford, came from a wool merchant family. In buying the main part of the estate for £1,600 and further local Hussey family lands for £1,800, by 1560 Ford had acquired substantial land with high commercial value in sheep, timber and iron forges at nearby West Harting and Nyewood.

On Ford's death in 1568, the estate was inherited and divided between his two daughters, Dorothy and Magdalen. The latter owned Uppark and it was probably her son, Sir William Ford (b.1571), who commissioned a house on the site by c.1595. Her grandson, Sir Edward Ford (1605–70), continued the family's support of the king, but in 1643 he was besieged in Arundel Castle, for which he still held an ancient feudal duty to defend, and was subsequently imprisoned in the Tower of London. Land confiscation was often a penalty but a good proportion of his Harting estates was spared, possibly due to the fact that his wife, Sarah Ireton, was the sister of the then Parliamentary general, Henry Ireton. As an engineer and inventor Sir Edward was also encouraged by Cromwell to devise a method for pumping water from the River Thames to the higher streets of London. Sir Edward's invention was not able to overcome the 310ft ascent to Uppark, and the house relied on water supplied from wells and dew-ponds until c.1731 when a 'Water Engine' is mentioned in the accounts.

Above *View of South Harting, Sussex* by Joseph Francis Gilbert (1792–1855), 1834. By the pond is the Engine House which pumped water up to the house. The Engine House still stands on the edge of South Harting village

The Tankervilles

The Right Hon:ble the Lord Grey.

P. Lelly Eques Pinxit. Sold by Alex: Browne at ỹ blew Ballcony in little Queen street.

Catherine Ford (1634–82) inherited Uppark from her father in 1670 and it was her son, from a second marriage to Ralph, 2nd Lord Grey of Warke (1630–75), who rebuilt the house we see today.

Ford, 3rd Lord Grey of Warke, Viscount Glendale and Earl of Tankerville (1655–1701), was described as 'a cowardly, perfidious person'. In 1682 he was brought to trial for 'conspiring, contriving, practising, and intending the final ruin of Henrietta Berkeley', his sister in-law, with whom he eloped. An ardent Protestant, Ford was deeply involved in the anti-Catholic movements against the monarchy led by the Duke of Monmouth, including the failed Rye House Plot (1683) to kidnap and assassinate Charles II and his brother, the future James II. He narrowly escaped imprisonment in the Tower of London by getting the sergeant-at-arms drunk on 14 bottles of claret, and fled in disguise to Uppark, then on to Vlissingen in the Netherlands via Chichester harbour. Ford went on to play a rather unsuccessful role as Monmouth's principal lieutenant; during the July 1685 rebellion his 'newly raised and undisciplined' cavalry were defeated. Captured by the king's forces, Ford turned on his fellow conspirators by providing evidence against them and bribing his judges.

Ford's fortunes changed in 1688 with the successful coup and ensuing reign of William III and Queen Mary. He was rewarded with a place on the Privy Council and the earldom of Tankerville. It was most likely during this period that Ford commissioned the building of the

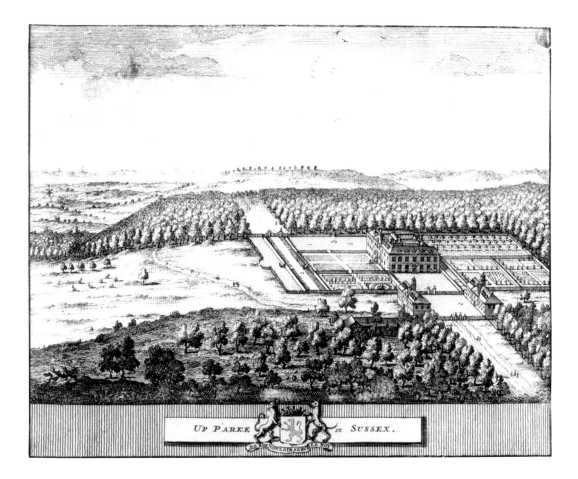

UP PARKE in SUSSEX.

current house in the fashionable Anglo-Dutch style. An engraving by Johannes Kip, in the 1707 publication *Britannia Illustrata,* shows the earliest image of the house and formal gardens which were described by the traveller and diarist Celia Fiennes as 'new built' in 1695. Uppark is one of the finest surviving examples of the tradition of brick country-house building, introduced to England from the Netherlands in the 1660s. The key features of the style are the simplicity and symmetry of the box-shaped form, hipped-roof with deep cornice, dormer windows in the roof, tall chimney stacks, and central three-bay section set forward with a pediment.

Though traditionally ascribed to William Talman, the architecture of the house as originally constructed is more in line with the simplicity of form by fellow architect Sir Hugh May.

Ford was able to enjoy his new house for only a short time as he died in 1701 when Uppark passed on to his only surviving child Mary (c.1678–1710), whose husband was made 1st Earl of Tankerville of the second creation. They don't appear to have spent much time at Uppark but their son Charles, 2nd Earl Tankerville (1697–1753), used it as a base for hunting and even commissioned before 1734 two impressive large paintings of the house and setting by the Flemish artist Pieter Tillemans.

Opposite The Right Hon. the Lord Grey in a print after Sir Peter Lely, published in 1707 by Alexander Browne who produced mezzotints in the 1680s, mostly based on Lely but also Van Dyck

Above left View of Uppark: Lord Tankerville's House and Formal Gardens by Johannes Kip after Leonard Knyff, as published in *Britannia Illustrata,* 1707

Sir Matthew and Sarah, Lady Fetherstonhaugh

Sir Matthew Fetherstonhaugh (1714–74) bought Uppark for £19,000 from Charles Tankerville in 1747, the same year he successfully petitioned for his baronetcy and just months after marrying Sarah, Lady Fetherstonhaugh (1722–88). A well-matched couple, Matthew came from a Northumbrian family whose money was acquired through the coal and wine trades, and Sarah was born into the wealthy, educated and influential Lethieullier family, descended from prominent London Huguenot merchants.

The couple enjoyed living life to the full, engaging in society pastimes; their account books reveal frequent spending on visits to the opera, dancing, fine clothes and gambling. Sarah was a proficient amateur artist, and three of her watercolours can be seen today in the Red Drawing Room. She brought to Uppark (or later commissioned) portraits of her family, important furniture and one of its treasures, a rare dolls' house made c.1735–40 (see pages 46–7). Sir Matthew was described as 'A gentleman of Literature and Improvement and versed in Natural Knowledge', fully immersed in social and political events. In 1755 he was elected a member of parliament for Morpeth, Northumberland, and then Portsmouth from 1761 until his death. He was one of the largest shareholders in Bank of England and East India Company stocks, giving him substantial influence in voting to expand British commercial territories by seizing land in India and parts of south-east Asia. Substantial investments were also made in the Grand Ohio Company which bought, by various means, land from the First Peoples of North America with the aim of forming new colonies.

Uppark was chosen as their country home, in part to satisfy Sir Matthew's inheritance which stipulated he must settle in the south of England. It was also only two days' carriage ride from London, a half-day ride to the coast, and close to members of Sarah's family in Hampshire. In the next decades the couple spent over £16,000 (around £1.8 million today) transforming the house. Sir Matthew's personal Account Book (1747–67) recorded 'On acct. of building at Uppark' payments for slating, glazing, plumbing, chimneypieces, plate, china and pictures. The architect initially involved may have been Daniel Garrett (d.1753), and the Account Book's mention of 'Paine' may refer to James Paine (1717–89) who was also commissioned to design their Whitehall house in 1754. Stylistically there is some evidence of Paine's hand in the ceilings of the Staircase Hall and the Red and Little Drawing Rooms. The Fetherstonhaughs added substantially to the existing contents, particularly during their Grand Tour of Europe (see page 10). Often groups of paintings were bought to hang in careful symmetry around grand mirrors and monumental marble chimneypieces. The influence of Sir Matthew and Sarah can still be seen today, even after later redecorations and restoration, particularly the architecture and furnishings in the Saloon and Little Parlour, reflecting the modern Neo-classical styles of the 1770s when a second phase of decoration was undertaken.

Clockwise from top left
Sir Matthew Fetherstonhaugh by William Hoare of Bath (1707–92), 1753. Pastel on paper

A Bay Horse in Landscape with his Groom and Two Hounds by William Shaw (fl.1755–c.1772), oil on canvas. In 1766 Matthew Fetherstonhaugh paid £27 6s for this and another painting by Shaw

Sarah, Lady Fetherstonhaugh by William Hoare of Bath, 1753. Pastel on paper. She is in 'Tyrolean' costume perhaps bought in the Alps during her Grand Tour. The portrait is in imitation of the 'fancy' pastels of Rosalba Carriera

A 'West Indian little black Monkey' with birds butterflies and flowers by Sarah, Lady Fetherstonhaugh, initialled and dated 1757. Watercolour on parchment

Top row, left to right
Sir Matthew Fetherstonhaugh, 1st Bt by Pompeo Batoni (1708–87), 1751

Katherine Durnford, Mrs Utrick Fetherstonhaugh by Pompeo Batoni, 1751

Lascelles Raymond Iremonger by Pompeo Batoni, 1751

Bottom row, left to right
Rev. Utrick Fetherstonhaugh by Pompeo Batoni, 1751

Sarah, Lady Fetherstonhaugh by Pompeo Batoni, 1751

The Grand Tour

The term 'Grand Tour' was first used by the writer and priest Richard Lassels in his guidebook *The Voyage of Italy* (published 1670) to describe the wealthy youth, usually accompanied by a mentor or tutor, travelling abroad to learn about international art and culture – sometimes in a broad sense.

By the 18th century, taking a Grand Tour over a number of years became *de rigueur* for those who could afford it, a way of bringing to life previous academic study and personal artistic interests. The historian, MP and friend of the Fetherstonhaughs, Edward Gibbon, once remarked that 'According to the law of custom, and perhaps of reason, foreign travel completes the education of an English gentleman'.

This travel experience was undertaken by women as well as men, and in 1749 Sarah, Lady Fetherstonhaugh and her husband embarked on their own Grand Tour of Europe. They were part of a group of family and friends comprising Sir Matthew's brother Utrick, Katherine Durnford (daughter of the vicar of Harting and later wife of Utrick), Sarah's brother, Benjamin Lethieullier, and half-brother, Lascelles Iremonger. The group followed the traditional route via France, crossing the Alps (carried by sedan-chair) at Mont Cenis before moving on to tour the major Italian cities including Florence, Venice and Rome. The group was observed as being 'vastly rich' and during their travels they did indeed spend money; Sir Matthew and Sarah acquired many works of art for Uppark, including in Rome a series of nine portraits of the group,

dated 1751 and 1752, and two subject paintings by the prominent Italian painter Pompeo Batoni (1708–87). Further purchases included two scagliola table-tops from the skilled Florentine craftsman-monk Don Petro Belloni at £25 and eight copies of views of Venice by Antonio Canaletto for £189 9s 9d. According to the fashionable French painter Joseph Vernet's order books, a 'M. Latheulier Anglais', presumably Benjamin Lethieullier, commissioned six marine pictures and landscapes at a cost of 600 Italian silver scudi in 1751. This group now hangs at Uppark and was probably bequeathed to Sir Harry Fetherstonhaugh on Benjamin's death in 1797. Sir Matthew and his Grand Tour party are also illustrated in Joshua Reynolds's 1751 satirical painting *Parody of Raphael's 'School of Athens'*.

In 1776, following his parents' lead, Sir Harry Fetherstonhaugh embarked on a Grand Tour of Europe with his uncle, now the Rev. Utrick Fetherstonhaugh. Together they visited Paris, Geneva, Venice, Florence, Rome and Naples. In Rome Sir Harry also sat for Batoni, and his portrait, with his mastiff dog beside him, now hangs in the Red Drawing Room. The Grand Tour experience was to give Sir Harry a lasting appreciation for, in particular, French arts and culture which influenced many of his subsequent purchases for Uppark.

Above Detail of *Parody of Raphael's 'School of Athens'* by Joshua Reynolds (1723–92), 1751. The painting caricatures mostly identifiable figures, including the Uppark party. The painting was commissioned by Joseph Henry of Straffan, County Kildare, who became 1st Earl of Milltown

Sir Harry Fetherstonhaugh

The Fetherstonhaugh's only child, Harry (1754–1846), was, according to his mother, 'born at Uppark on December 22nd 1754 at half an hour past ten in the morning'. No expense was spared on Harry's care and comfort. The account books included a number of purchases for the boy including buttons (£1 11s 6d), gloves (3s), hair cut (5s), pocket watch (15 guineas), accompanying chain & key (7s 6d) and 'Harry's horse' (£1 15s).

On Sir Matthew's death in 1774, Harry inherited not only the baronetcy but also £18,602 (around £1.6 million today) in debts, plus legal fees. To address the initial debts on the estate, the family sold shares in the East India Company, timber stocks, land in Essex and some property in London. His mother and uncle were entrusted with the care of Harry until he turned 21, the following year, at which point he was content for his mother to continue managing his personal accounts. The family purse was further stretched by his own spending. Edward Gibbon noted in 1775 that 'Sir Harry is very civil and good-humoured. But from the unavoidable temper of youth, I fear he will cost many a tear to Lady F.' Over just a few months in 1778 Sarah

Left *Sir Harry Fetherstonhaugh, 2nd Bt* by Pompeo Batoni (1708–87), 1776 discovered her son had spent £3,324 (about £286,000 today), and the following year the Fetherstonhaugh ancestral home in Northumberland was sold.

Sir Harry acquired much of the French decorative art at Uppark, and his informed aesthetic judgement was much valued, helping the Prince Regent acquire works of art in Paris. By the 1780s Sir Harry was firmly part of the royal circle and hosted numerous parties at Uppark (see page 18). By 1810 he had, for some unknown reason, fallen from favour and was no longer invited to the various gatherings. It seems to have affected him deeply and he wrote on his exclusion: 'I don't hug myself on not being one of them'. Sir Harry's time was now focused on Uppark and around this time he commissioned Humphry Repton to make alterations to the gardens and interiors.

Sir Harry had relationships with various women throughout his life, most famously Emma Hamilton (see page 18) but on 12 September 1825, in the Saloon at Uppark, aged 70 he married his 20-year-old dairymaid. Mary Ann Bullock (1805–74) had moved to the Uppark estate in her late teens, joining a team of dairymaids producing milk and butter products for the house. According to tradition,

Sir Harry walked past the dairy one day and, on hearing Mary Ann's singing voice, asked his servant to marry him. Society was quick to judge; the social commentator and diarist Harriet Arbuthnot wrote to the Duke of Wellington:

'I hear Sir Harry Fetherstonhaugh is to marry his cook!'

According to the gamekeeper, Mr Legge, even Sir Harry said he had 'made a fool' of himself. Yet despite any regret, prejudice and opposition, the marriage appears to have been a happy one and lasted over twenty years until Sir Harry's death in 1846.

Right A Sèvres (hard paste) *vase du roi, c.*1776, modelled in relief and gilt with swags of flowers, probably acquired by Sir Harry Fetherstonhaugh

Mary Ann, Lady Fetherstonhaugh and Frances Fetherstonhaugh

For almost three decades Mary Ann, Lady Fetherstonhaugh, whose own arms were registered with the College of Heralds, managed the estate with her younger sister Frances (1819–95). The period has been described as a 'long Victorian afternoon', preserved 'as Sir 'Arry 'ad it' yet the evidence shows a different story.

Family records reveal purchases of furniture, carpets and upholstery, along with notes referring to extensive repainting of the principal rooms and reglazing of many sash windows. Much of the work related to necessary maintenance and adapting Uppark to modern technology, such as boiler and stove replacements, but a number of the rooms were redecorated with fashionable 1850s 'Satin flock' or 'mauve and crimson figured stripe Merino damask' wall coverings. Mary Ann appears to have shared her husband's taste for French decorative arts, experiencing the culture first hand. Soon after her marriage, Mary Ann went to Paris to improve her education, and in 1847, a year after Sir Harry's death, she travelled with her sister Frances, her agent and two servants to Paris, and the palaces at Fontainebleau and Versailles.

Right Mary Ann, Lady Fetherstonhaugh, who married Sir Harry in 1825, photographed c.1860

'It is a very good thing, to be a downstairs person as well as an upstairs person.'

Mary Ann, Lady Fetherstonhaugh

Understanding the advantages in her life, she was reportedly a fair landowner. At Christmas, gifts were laid out for the servants and inhabitants of South Harting, including 'piles of red flannel petticoats and mounds of red rounds of beef and Christmas pies and puddings'. She also kept Sir Harry's tradition of hospitality; during her time, Uppark was the venue for social events, winter shooting parties and even friends' honeymoons: the 2nd Lord and Lady Leconfield (of Petworth) in 1867 and the 5th Earl and Countess Winterton (of Shillinglee Park) in 1882.

Both Mary Ann and Frances were generous donors to local charities, including the local school in South Harting, and established the 'Frances Bullock Fetherstonhaugh Charity for Poor Men'. Mary Ann died in 1874, leaving Uppark to Frances who took the name Fetherstonhaugh. Frances donated to Harting Church in memory of her close friend Ann Sutherland, the presumed illegitimate daughter of Sir Harry, who lived at Uppark until her death in 1893. By their later years the friends were said to have 'always dressed in velvet as they thought it suited the house best'.

Frances Fetherstonhaugh died two years later and, understandably, there was much speculation as to who would inherit Uppark. Considerable research had been undertaken to find a legitimate blood heir of Sir Harry, to no avail. She finally left Uppark to Lt Col the Hon. Keith Turnour (1848–1930), the younger son of her close friends, the 4th Earl and Countess Winterton.

Top The house from the north east, c.1890

Bottom Frances Fetherstonhaugh (centre) seated with guests, including Col Keith Turnour-Fetherstonhaugh (far right), on the south steps of Uppark

The last private owners

Col Keith Turnour-Fetherstonhaugh's ownership of Uppark is captured in a *Country Life* article of 1910 showing the paintings hung in the same places as early 19th-century plans. Absent are important pieces of French works of art sold by the family to the London art dealers Partridge, for £38,000, the following year. The sales were probably necessary for the upkeep of the house and estate, but it was also suggested by the then Lord Tankerville that 'a host of lovely things had been lost over a game of cards'.

In 1930 Admiral the Hon. Sir Herbert Meade-Fetherstonhaugh (1875–1964) inherited Uppark, as stipulated by Miss Fetherstonhaugh's will. The Admiral had had a distinguished service on destroyers during the First World War, and later as Admiral Commanding Royal Yachts. His obituary described him as 'that splendid mixture of sailor and courtier epitomised by Marrat in the term "sea gentleman".' In 1911 he married Margaret Glyn (1888–1977) who recorded the 'marked kindness of many happy visits to Colonel Keith Turnour-Fetherstonhaugh and his daughter'. Uppark had a deep impression on Lady Meade-Fetherstonhaugh:

'Among my first impressions colour and light shone in an unbroken tranquillity of peace, which impressed and held one.'

Above Margaret, Lady Meade-Fetherstonhaugh and her daughter Jean showing two Uppark curtains before (right) and after (left) their conservation work, *c*.1935

Above right The Saloon, photographed *c*.1910

Opposite Admiral the Hon. Sir Herbert Meade-Fetherstonhaugh, and Margaret, Lady Meade-Fetherstonhaugh with their dog on the Saloon steps, *c*.1955

When the Meade-Fetherstonhaughs moved to Uppark in 1931, after 'twenty years in twenty houses' they were determined to make it a family home, entering the 'fairy story' of their lives. They undertook major repairs to the property, which had suffered from lack of investment since Miss Fetherstonhaugh's time. Lady Meade-Fetherstonhaugh was 'the visionary behind … the complete reinstatement of the building to its former glory'. Margaret embarked on many years of conservation work, becoming internationally respected for her work with textiles. Often involving family and friends, tasks included pulling curtains over dewy grass to wet them or immersion in soapwort-infused water to clean the silk fibres. Evidence of Margaret's conservation work can be seen all around Uppark and she chronicled the various projects in her diaries, keeping samples of fabrics used

and replaced, so that much was learned about the collection through her work. By the time of the 1989 fire, many of the once-threadbare curtains were over-sewn with 'tram-lines' and strong enough to be pulled down in one piece by firefighters. From the 1950s her skills were sought after, and textiles were sent for repair to Uppark from Britain, the Continent and America.

In 1954 Admiral Sir Herbert Meade-Featherstonhaugh and his eldest son Richard gave Uppark, with land to protect its setting, to the National Trust. After the deaths of her son Richard in 1958 and her husband in 1964, Lady Meade-Fetherstonhaugh continued to live at Uppark until 1965 when she passed the tenancy to her widowed daughter-in-law Jean Meade-Fetherstonhaugh. Subsequent generations of the Meade-Fetherstonhaugh family continue to call Uppark their home.

Guests at Uppark

Uppark, in common with most country houses, has had a long tradition of hospitality, though most publicly during Sir Harry's time when guests included the Prince of Wales (later King George IV) and his entourage.

His second visit in 1785 required the elderly Sarah, Lady Fetherstonhaugh and her niece, Elizabeth Iremonger, to vacate their rooms to make space for the 'Prince and his Party'. Elizabeth wrote:

'The entertainment was to last three days; great preparations were making [sic] to render it completely elegant; Races of all sorts were to be upon the most beautiful Spot of Ground I believe that England can produce.'

Sir Harry and his guests raced horses for money and a silver-gilt trophy inscribed 'The Prince's Cup Uppark 1785' is now on display in the Dining Room and Servery.

One of the most famous guests during this period was the girl who would later become Lady Hamilton (1765–1815). In 1780, aged just 15, Emma Hart, as she was then known, met Sir Harry at the 'Temple of Health and Hymen' in London, where it is thought she worked as an entertainer. Navigating 18th-century society using her considerable intellect and charm, Emma was often the subject of cruel gossip, including the tradition that she danced naked on the dining table at Uppark. The nature of Emma's relationship with Sir Harry is not entirely clear due to lack of historical evidence, but she did live on the Uppark Estate and was part of many social gatherings at the house. In the winter of 1781, six months pregnant, Emma was sent away from Uppark to her home county of Cheshire.

Above *The Prince Regent* after John Russell (1745–1806), c.1790. The pastel on paper hangs at Antony House, Cornwall

Sir Harry was assumed to be the father and Emma wrote numerous times for his help. In a letter to his friend Charles Greville, she wrote:

'What shall I dow? I have wrote 7 letters, and no anser .... What else am I but a girl in distress – in real distress.'

She survived this crisis but later in life, falling again on hard times, she wrote to Sir Harry who did reply this time: 'No one better deserves to be happy'. He sent money and invited her to return 'dans la belle saison' but sadly she never saw Uppark again.

Right The writer H. G. Wells by Sir William Rothenstein (1872–1945)

Below *Emma Hamilton* by George Romney (1734–1802), *c.*1785. Emma Hamilton became Romney's muse, inspiring or informing over 60 paintings

During his youth, the writer H. G. Wells (1866–1946) stayed a number of times at Uppark where his mother, Sarah, was housekeeper between 1880 and 1893. His biography includes important memories of his time at Uppark, reading books from the library and stargazing through his telescope from his attic bedroom. His creative imagination was informed by his experiences at Uppark:

'there was a great snowstorm which snowed me up for nearly a fortnight, and I produced a daily newspaper of a facetious character, The Uppark Alarmist – on what was properly kitchen paper – and gave a shadow play to the maids and others, in a miniature theatre I made in the housekeeper's room.'

Uppark had an enduring impact on Wells and the house was the inspiration for 'Bladesover' in his novel *Tono-Bungay* (1909).

Servants

No country house could function without servants, and the census for 1841 records over 68 servants living at Uppark and the following census lists a total of 203 servants, many living in the surrounding area, employed by 'Dame Mary Anne Fetherstonhaugh'.

Uppark was powered by these people working in various 'engine-rooms' within the basement, service buildings and wider estate. Here food was grown and prepared, horses and carriages looked after, meals cooked, tableware cleaned and stored, laundry washed and ironed. A number of duties were carried out 'above-stairs', some in clear sight of the family such as waiting at the dining table or dressing the master, others out-of-sight such as laying fires, cleaning and changing bedlinen. Servants were summoned on demand via a system of bells installed c.1800. After c.1815 the house was connected to the service blocks by the underground tunnels which created an effective means of communication to ensure things ran smoothly. The servants came together for meals but ate according to their rank either in the Steward's Hall (for upper servants) or the Servants' Hall. The house servants slept in the attic, with a separate stair for access to the family rooms, while grooms slept above the stables. The butler and housekeeper had their own rooms in the basement from 1704, reflecting their status as the head of household and head of staff

Above Christmas lunch in the Servants' Hall, 1936. From left (seated facing) Lilian the lady's maid, Gwendoline Coakes opposite her husband William, the chauffeur, and far right Alma White, housemaid and daughter of Tinny White, a gamekeeper

respectively. Those in roles such as valet, lady's maid and coachman often travelled with the family, their duties tied to the personal needs of their employers. In Sir Matthew and Sarah, Lady Fetherstonhaugh's lifetime, 28 indoor and 15 outdoor servants moved between their London house and Uppark.

Some servants were employed at Uppark for most of their lives, including Thomas Deller who was Sir Harry's butler for 50 years and portrayed in a drawing by C. H. Tatham of 1806. Others worked at Uppark multiple times such as Sarah Wells (1822–1905). She began her career at the house in 1850 as maid for Frances Fetherstonhaugh. Sarah developed a close bond with her mistress and reluctantly left her post in 1853 to marry Joseph Wells, a former Uppark gardener, and move to Bromley, Kent. They had four children – the youngest, 'Bertie', grew up to be the famous writer H. G. Wells. Returning to Uppark in 1880, Sarah took up the position of housekeeper. According to her son, Sarah 'knew at least how a housekeeper should look, and assumed a lace cap, lace apron, black silk dress and all the rest of it' but had no

Sarah 'knew at least how a housekeeper should look, and assumed a lace cap, lace apron, black silk dress and all the rest of it' H. G. Wells

experience of such a demanding role. Sarah was accommodated by Frances for almost 13 years before 'the rather sentimental affection between them evaporated' and she was asked to leave.

At times, some of the owners of Uppark were themselves in service to others. Camilla, Lady Tankerville (1698–1775), was appointed Lady of the Bedchamber to Queen Caroline.

Above Mrs Sarah Wells (b.1822), housekeeper at Uppark from 1880 to 1893 and mother of the writer H. G. Wells

Left Thomas Deller by C. H. Tatham, 1806. Deller was Sir Harry's butler for over 50 years

The Fire

Fire has been dreaded by country-house owners for centuries, to the point of influencing their layout and design. Houses can be at their most vulnerable during building work, and so it was with Uppark.

On 30 August 1989 the house was covered in scaffolding towards the end of a year-long programme of structural and roof repairs. At 3.36pm the alarm sounded when fire broke out in the roof where workmen had been repairing leadwork. The fire brigade was quick to respond with an engine on site within 15 minutes, but it swiftly became evident that it was impossible to prevent the fire spreading and that it might engulf the whole house.

The Sussex Deputy Chief Fire Officer, Kenneth Lloyd, made the decision to concentrate efforts towards buying time for his teams to support the rescue of the contents. In total 27 fire engines and 156 fire personnel attended and helped National Trust staff, volunteers and members of the Meade-Fetherstonhaugh family in saving furniture, textiles and works of art before the flames reached them. Sadly, such was the speed of the fire, the upper floors had to be abandoned at an early stage and the family lost almost all of their privately owned items. From the show rooms and basement, human chains were formed to retrieve what could be saved, samples of wall coverings were taken and the fire brigade braved hazardous conditions in rescuing paintings, such as the Tillemans landscapes next to the burning staircase and three large rococo pier-glasses, one still on fire as it was handed through the window. By evening the house was deemed too dangerous to enter and people could only watch in dismay as the flames engulfed the house and contents. The next morning only the shell of the building remained but miraculously some of the contents had survived for salvage, such as the 'Prince Regent's Bed' in the Tapestry Bedroom, which was retrieved just before the ceiling collapsed, and the Axminster carpet in the Red Drawing Room which was discovered, with only partial loss, three days after the fire.

In the following weeks and months, a systematic, archaeological approach led to further salvage of damaged and fragmented items. The decision was taken to restore Uppark to the day before the fire 'in so far as was practical'. The recent maintenance works had provided much information about the house, and it was soon discovered that the fabric of the building and much of the wall decoration on the ground floor had survived intact, together with more than 90 per cent of the furnishings for the show rooms. Uppark was restored, setting new standards for the conservation of fire-damaged historic buildings, and reopened to the public in 1995, at the heart of the National Trust's centenary celebrations.

Left Uppark on fire from the south east

Right Fire damage in the Saloon, taken on 11 September 1989

Left Anne King, a free-hand stucco plasterer, working on the Red Drawing Room ceiling

Craftspeople

Uppark has been described as a 'virtuoso monument to the British genius for craftsmanship'. From its creation, Uppark has built upon generations of craftsmanship, from the interiors to the landscaped gardens.

When the Meade-Fetherstonhaugh family inherited Uppark in 1930, they undertook major repairs to the property as documented in photographs taken of some of the skilled workers, including roofers and stonemasons. Over the following decades they dedicated their lives to bring back its furnishings and fabrics to their original 18th-century condition.

The most significant period of craftsmanship for Uppark was following the fire in 1989 until reopening in 1995. The £20 million restoration project required the work of specialist craftspeople, drawing on their expertise and, in many cases, reviving historic techniques and learning new skills. The building was made whole again with a new slate roof, 'bossed' leadwork, and hand-thrown chimney-pots by West Meon Pottery, while window panes were sourced from a French manufacturer of hand-blown *verre royale* glass.

In total 12,000 fragments from the inside of the house were carefully assessed, inventoried and stored. From them the team had pieces of a puzzle to put back together and in most cases combine with new parts. The ceilings are a prime example of this work where craft skills were revived on a scale not undertaken in England for over 150 years. A team of ten plasterers was appointed and painstakingly learnt the technique of free-hand modelling in lime plaster directly on to the ceiling. The results are triumphant in replicating the form and liveliness of the original ceilings in the show rooms. The redecoration of the interiors was toned to match the remaining paintwork, and the furnishings and contents of the show rooms were carefully restored where possible.

Works of art have also been fully recreated. In the Staircase Hall sits a faithful reconstruction of a pier table dating from c.1747 (destroyed in the fire and pair to another on display in the Servery), completed in 2013 by the conservator and restorer Peter Thuring with funds from the Monument Trust.

The restoration of Uppark shows very clearly that craft is far from dead. In his 1995 introduction to *Uppark Restored,* Martin Drury, then Director-General of the National Trust, wrote: 'Visitors to Uppark today can see the work of craftsmen and women of the 1990s beside that of their eighteenth-century predecessors and they are indistinguishable. The truth is that the skills exist or are latent; all that is needed is the will, and the money to pay for them.'

Right The door architraves of the Saloon have 'capitals' of serpents by James Paine. The original carving of c.1770 can be seen alongside the restored c.1995 sections

A Tour of Uppark

Uppark sits proudly atop the South Downs ridge with views south across to the coast. It is the only country house in the area that occupies such a prime position, being seen for miles around, reflecting its importance and the long history of human habitation at Uppark.

The landscape around Uppark remains largely forested with the house appearing within a secluded open space on the ridge. When the house was first built in the 17th century, the principal approach was from the east, along a driveway that provided views of the house long before arrival between two earlier service blocks. The tourist and writer Celia Fiennes described it in 1695 as:

'Square, with nine windows in the front and seven in the sides, brickwork with free stone coyness and windows, in the midst of fine gardens, gravell [sic] and grass walks and bowling green.'

Despite its attributes, not everyone has felt Uppark looks as impressive as it should. Repton commented that it resembled more a 'shooting box of a Woodland Country, than the Palace worthy of so proved a situation'. Today, at Repton's suggestion, the house and grounds are approached from historic entrance drives through woodland, via a set of 'golden gates' and along an avenue of trees. Although not linked together by colonnades, as Repton had proposed, the grouping of buildings, driveway turning circle, foliage and planting sets the house on its own pedestal. In the 1880s visitors would have been greeted by peacocks fond of roosting on ball finials to the gate piers.

Left The square piers and gates at the north entrance created by Humphry Repton c.1810

Opposite The north drive leading to Repton's Portland stone portico is planted with Norway maples (Acer platanoïdes)

The house fronts

Above **Repton's north-front colonnade.** He specified 'a quiet not a paper white' for the front door

The many approaches and arrival points that have existed over the centuries have given the house not one but three entrance fronts.

The north front

Today the principal entrance to the house, this front predominantly comprises a Portland stone portico of Tuscan (plain and undecorated) columns designed and erected by Humphry Repton c.1811–14. The front door, painted 'a quiet not a paper white', works harmoniously with the stuccoed walls of the portico which, over time, have become beautifully embellished with a growth of lichen.

The east front

This was originally the main entrance to the house until construction of Repton's new north front. As shown in the Knyff and Kip engraving of 1695–1701, this entrance was framed within two gated courtyards between the original service buildings and led into the Stone Hall.

The south front

This is still the principal and most impressive façade of the house, facing the best views across the downs and a perfect backdrop to social gatherings. Constructed c.1690 for Lord Grey, the design is traditionally ascribed to William Talman, although the architectural style is more in line with the simplicity of form by fellow architect Sir Hugh May. Despite its solid and unmolested appearance, this front has gone through a number of alterations; in the 18th century the Grey achievement of arms (a full display of the owner's heraldic bearings) was replaced with those of Sir Matthew Fetherstonhaugh, the depth of the windows was increased and sashes were replaced, some reused as roof joists. In turn the 18th-century sashes were almost all replaced by Lady Fetherstonhaugh in 1865 with four-pane plate-glass windows. Subsequent restorations by the National Trust have returned the windows to the 18th-century style. The brickwork on all three fronts was largely undamaged by the fire of 1989 but repairs have been made and continue to be needed, and several stone window architraves have been replaced.

Multiple entrances

The succession of entrance fronts has been reflected in the internal spaces into which they led, each change forcing a reappraisal of the room and its contents.

North Corridor

The north-front portico entrance leads into a series of airy spaces comprising the North Corridor. Designed by Repton c.1811–14 it remains as first intended, having been repainted after the fire in the original stone paint colour. The skylights were supplied by the firm of Underwood & Doyle, specialist manufacturers and 'Stained-Glass-Painters' whose work can also be seen in the London home of the architect Sir John Soane.

The mahogany hall chairs (c.1790) and benches (c.1815) are all decorated with the Fetherstonhaugh arms, and a carving over the doorway, probably bought by Sir Harry on his Grand Tour, bears the arms of the Order of the Knights of St John.

Staircase Hall

This grand space occupies the centre of the house and forms the primary link between the social spaces on the ground floor and the private family rooms above. Visitors would have arrived in the adjacent Stone Hall or gathered in the Saloon to be greeted by the family as they descended the stairs.

Until the fire, which burnt fiercest here, the panelling and staircase woodwork were original to the Tankerville house, c.1690; now they are replaced by faithful copies except for two original sections including the newel post at the base of the stair. The space was probably remodelled by the architect James Paine around

Stone Hall

Until the portico entrance was built on the north front, this was the day-to-day entrance to the house. This function is reflected in the practical stone floor (hence the name of the room) and large fireplace to warm those coming in from the cold. The green paint colour was restored after the fire, based on an inventory description of 1814, a fragment of which can be seen to the right of the fireplace. The white marble fireplace dates from the first phase of Sir Matthew and Sarah, Lady Fetherstonhaugh's redecoration in the 1750s. The carved decoration features children garlanding a goat flanked by sphinxes (after designs by James Paine the Elder) and was probably supplied by Thomas Carter the Elder.

Displayed here are portraits of family members including Admiral the Hon. Sir Herbert Meade-Fetherstonhaugh (who inherited Uppark in 1931) from an original by Sir Oswald Birley in 1940.

1750, the Venetian-style window and ceiling plasterwork being similar to Paine's work at Wadsworth Hall, Yorkshire. The pink-and-white paintwork is a restoration of an early 19th-century scheme.

At the foot of the stairs hang two huge landscape paintings by Pieter Tillemans (1684–1734) showing the bird's-eye *View of Uppark* and *View on the Downs near Uppark,* both commissioned by the 2nd Earl of Tankerville in the 1720s. On the west wall hang portraits of Sir Matthew and Sarah, Lady Fetherstonhaugh, painted by William Hoare of Bath (1707–92), probably painted when the couple visited the city in 1753.

On the table sit gilt bronzes by Pierre-François Feuchière (1737–1823), based on larger equine sculptures made for the royal park of Marly outside Paris, and today housed in the Louvre Museum.

The east rooms

Repton's Servery was added to facilitate the final touches to dishes before they were taken to the table; until the Kitchen was brought into the house after 1895, food had to be brought along the basement passages.

Dining Room and Servery

In 1705 the space was divided into 'My Lords Bedchamber' and 'The Parlor Next'. It is unclear when the two rooms became one but Humphry Repton appears to have been responsible for the cohesive interior scheme of *c*.1812–13. The north wall of the Servery, visible to guests, is decorated with a central stained-glass panel designed by the architect's son John Adey Repton.

The dining table is laid with a Chinese export dinner service, *c*.1765, with the arms of Sir Matthew Fetherstonhaugh impaling those of his wife, Sarah Lethieullier. The porcelain centrepiece, 'Autumn', was made by the Sèvres factory in 1816 and bought by Sir Harry.

Guests of Sir Harry feasted on the superb cuisine of his French chef, Monsieur Moget. In 1784, fare for the Prince Regent and guests included '2 Bucks. A Welsh sheep, a doz. Ducks, – 4 Hams, dozens of Pigeons, and Rabbits, Flitches of Bacon, Lobsters and Prawns; a Turtle of 120 lbs.' along with wine, beer, brandy and port. The three-day party required 'another chef to assist Moget' at a cost of £25.

Above One of a pair of silver canisters by the silversmiths William Vincent and John Lawford, London, 1767

Below left Repton's Servery is illuminated by a window designed by his son, John Adey

Below right The Dining Room, looking towards the Stone Hall

On the west wall hangs a set of paintings by Claude-Joseph Vernet (1714–89) depicting the Four Times of Day, commissioned in 1751 by Benjamin Lethieullier, brother to Sarah, Lady Fetherstonhaugh, during their Grand Tour.

Little Parlour

This room is best placed for morning and afternoon light, being on the south-east corner of the house, and was popular with the women of Uppark. In the 19th century Frances Fetherstonhaugh and Ann Sutherland 'spent whole days in the parlour … between reading and slumber and caressing their two pet dogs'.

The Neo-classical-style plasterwork ceiling, created c.1770, was almost completely destroyed by a falling chimneystack in 1989. Miraculously all but one of the ceiling medallions survived in the rubble and were restored to their original locations within the new plasterwork. The green wall paint follows the post-1814 scheme also adopted in the adjacent Stone Hall. A fragment of Chinese wallpaper decorated with birds and flowers survives from an earlier scheme of the 1750s.

The two overdoor portraits are of Sir Matthew and Sarah, Lady Fetherstonhaugh, painted in Rome in 1751 by the fashionable artist Pompeo Batoni.

On the table in the centre of the room is a pair of silver canisters by the silversmiths William Vincent and John Lawford, London, 1767. These rare circular tea canisters bear the arms of Sir Matthew and Sarah, Lady Fetherstonhaugh, and would have been part of a set including teapots and a kettle, also in silver.

Above left The Little Parlour has a wooden chimneypiece with a carved head of Bacchus, probably by James Paine c.1750

Above right A fragment of the Chinese hand-painted wallpaper which decorated the Little Parlour in the 1750s

Saloon

This room was originally the formal entrance hall of the Tankerville house, leading through to the Staircase Hall, furnished in 1705 with 'Eighteen Dutch Chaires two long mats' and called the 'Greate hall'. The space was much taller, taking in the mezzanine floor above where the Print Room was added c.1770 when the Fetherstonhaughs created the present Saloon.

Arguably one of the most beautiful saloons in Neo-classical style in Britain and probably designed by James Paine, it made the perfect setting for Sir Harry's marriage to Mary Ann,

Lady Fetherstonhaugh, on 12 September 1825. The gold-and-white gilded and painted walls (now faded to a softer grey) were decorated accorded to Humphry Repton's scheme of c.1814.

They survived the fire to allow the restored and newly made plasterwork and woodwork to be matched. The top right and lower left of the west doorcase have been left unpainted to show both the original and new carving.

At each end of the room are monumental fireplaces, made by Thomas Carter's London workshop c.1750. The marble sculptural decoration depicts the stories of *Romulus and Remus* (west) and *Androcles and the Lion* (east). Hanging above are Nathanial Dance's portraits of George III and Queen Charlotte, shown at the first Royal Academy of Arts exhibition in London in 1769. Dance also painted the overdoor portrait of the young Sir Harry Fetherstonhaugh as a hunter. Flanking the central north door are two biblical scenes from the *Prodigal Son* cycle, painted by the Italian artist Luca Giordano in the 1680s.

The best of Sir Harry's French furniture is in the Saloon, including four pedestals attributed to André-Charles Boulle, cabinetmaker to Louis XIV and master of the technique of inlaid brass, pewter and turtle shell. In the centre right of the room is a writing table or *bureau plat* made in 1715–23, supporting a small bookcase and a clock in the form of the Greek god Apollo. The early 19th-century gilt-bronze chandelier hanging in the centre of the room crashed to the floor during the fire but was remarkably undamaged and the gilding is original.

The bookcases were added by Repton c.1814 and house the main library at Uppark. They were used by Sir Harry Fetherstonhaugh for his collection of over 300 books.

Opposite above The Saloon. Over the east fireplace is Nathaniel Dance's portrait of George III

Opposite below The Romulus and Remus plaque on the west chimneypiece

Above left *The Son taking leave of his Father* by Luca Giordano (1632–1705)

Above right Detail of a Boulle pedestal

Drawing Rooms

The name 'drawing room' derives from the 16th-century 'withdrawing' room or chamber, semi-private spaces where hosts and privileged guests could withdraw. By the 18th century these rooms were being used in a similar way to modern-day living rooms, to receive and entertain family and friends. As Elizabeth Iremonger commented in 1786, '… every evening my Piano forte takes its share with the two violins, & we form a Concert which, I think, a delightful rational amusement.'

Red Drawing Room

Called the 'Great Parlor' in 1705, this room was where the Tankerville and Fetherstonhaugh families would have eaten. When the Dining Room was created, it then became the main Drawing Room,

The Red Drawing Room takes its name from the crimson flock wallpaper that has been used to decorate the walls since the mid-18th century. During the evacuation of contents in the 1989 fire, samples of this paper were torn from the walls to provide essential information for restoration. Today the wallpaper in this room is a combination of these and new sections made to match.

Between the windows sit a pair of commodes (or low cupboards) of c.1760–5. The front and sides are veneered with Chinese lacquer panels depicting scenes of palace life with figures in

Above The Red Drawing Room with the Carlton House-style mahogany writing table of c.1790 in the foreground, by tradition a gift from the Prince of Wales to Sir Harry

gardens and on terraces. In 2016–17 the commodes were conserved, repairing extensive cracks to the lacquer panels and historic damage to the carving and gilding, and returned to their intended appearance.

Sir Harry Fetherstonhaugh painted by Pompeo Batoni, dated 1776, hangs above the fireplace. It is the last in a series of paintings commissioned from Batoni by the Fetherstonhaughs (other examples can be seen in this room) during the traditional Grand Tour.

Sir Harry is shown with his mastiff dog whose collar bears the middle seven letters of his owner's name. Below the portrait hangs Sir Harry's walking stick, used in his old age as he suffered terribly with gout.

Little Drawing Room

Originally used as a smaller, more intimate space, by 1874 it had become the Dressing Room for the adjoining Tapestry Bedroom.

In 1705 the decoration was luxurious with 'Fine Guilt Leather' on the walls. The ceiling, woodwork and pelmets were installed by Sir Matthew c.1750. These were severely damaged in the fire and today the decoration is largely a restoration.

The impressive giltwood mirror between the windows was made c.1752 in the fashionable *Chinoiserie* style. It is the most important of the mirrors at Uppark, still in its original condition thanks to rescue, in one piece, by firemen in 1989.

On the cabinet is an example of 'upcycling'. The potpourri vase and cover, as now intended, comprises a 1761 Sèvres porcelain chamberpot on a pedestal base with a porcelain cupid forming the lid. The ensemble is mounted in gilt-bronze, with some additional decoration, probably by the London dealer E. H. Baldock to meet British demand for Sèvres porcelain objects in the early 19th century.

Above The Little Drawing Room. Above the cabinet is another of Luca Giordano's cycle of six paintings on the theme of the prodigal son, *The Fatted Calf*

Right A vase and cover formed around a 1761 Sèvres chamberpot. Such unusual creations were made for wealthy 19th-century collectors

Tapestry Bedroom and Flower Room

In the 17th century, when Uppark was built, houses usually had some bedrooms on the ground floor and the use of this 'Best Bedchamber' remained until _c._1910 when it became a sitting room. Later it became Admiral Meade-Fetherstonhaugh's room in which a television was installed on his 80th birthday in 1956.

Today the room is restored as a bedroom and the walls are hung with a set of three early 18th-century Flemish tapestries, inspired by

Below The Tapestry Bedroom is hung with Flemish early 18th-century tapestries inspired by David Teniers the Younger (1610–90): this depicts the barrelling of wine

scenes from David Teniers the Younger depicting village and harvest scenes, hand-woven in workshops run by Urbain and Daniel Leyniers, and Peter van den Hecke. They were bought back for Uppark, having been sold by the family in the early 20th century, by an anonymous benefactor after the fire, from a bank in Chicago which had bought them in 1972.

The bed was put together after _c._1760 and comprises early 17th-century giltwood putti and 18th-century parts. Sarah, Lady Fetherstonhaugh probably brought the canopy, tester cloth, head cloth and bedspread from another bed of _c._1720–30. Until the late 20th century the bed stood in the Prince Regent's Room upstairs, and it was presumably this bed that was used by the Prince during his visits in 1795 and 1796. When he later wrote to Sir Harry, inviting himself for another stay, he refers to 'my old Bed at Up Park'.

On the fireplace sits a garniture of three Sèvres jardinières, made in 1774. They are probably the set ordered from the factory in 1773 by Marie Antoinette, being decorated with her arms and those of her husband, Louis XVI (as Dauphin).

Flower Room

In 1705 this was 'the Closet Next [the Best Bedchamber]' and provided an en-suite room for washing and dressing. By the 1870s it had become a bathroom before becoming a room where cut-flower decorations for the house were prepared – hence the current name.

The Tapestry
Bedroom

Print Room

This room, occasionally open to visitors, is one of a series of three created when the mezzanine floor above the Saloon was installed by Sir Matthew Fetherstonhaugh *c.*1770. Later, from 1931, Admiral Meade-Fetherstonhaugh used this room as a dressing room and it was in a prime position for him to scan the Solent with his telescope.

Print rooms appeared in Britain and Europe *c.*1750 and were created by pasting engravings onto backing paper and applying them to the walls to create a miniature picture gallery. Prints were very popular items, often depicting copies of famous paintings and, with the separate framing elements, many London print shops were established to supply collectors, manufacturers and decorators.

The prints at Uppark seem to have been applied to the walls at the same time the room was constructed. In the Uppark records there is a reference to £51 5s (over £4,000 today) being paid to 'Mrs Vivaro for Prints' in 1774. The prints are mostly after Italian, Flemish and Spanish Old Master paintings along with some contemporary examples, including a print after a Joshua Reynolds

painting of the actor *David Garrick between Tragedy and Comedy*. The cut-out watercolours of flowers in terracotta pots, below the border, were added later, probably in the early 19th century.

The Print Room structure was completely destroyed in the 1989 fire. By a very lucky coincidence, however, the prints and their straw-coloured backing paper had been removed for conservation, so it was possible to put them back when the room was restored.

Above **Print Room**

Left Detail of the cut-out watercolours of flowers in terracotta pots beneath the Print Room border

Basement and Servants' Hall

The basement was where most of the servants' activity took place and served as the 'engine-room' powering the house. Where possible, the rooms have been redecorated and refurnished since the fire in accordance with an inventory dating from 1874. Following the footprint of the house above, the corridors of the basement link the various spaces of activity with the underground passages and inner courtyard, facilitating access to numerous points of entry to the floors above.

Servants' Hall

The Servants' Hall accommodated the majority of servants for their daily meals. They were seated in strict order of status, with the most junior members nearest the door where draughts would have been felt – although the closeness to the fire would have somewhat compensated, it was probably their job to maintain it. Strict rules would have been in place to control behaviour but that's not to say fun was not had. H. G. Wells wrote of his time at Uppark: 'below stairs was gay at Christmas and I was gay with it'. Special holidays would have been celebrated in modest ways with decorations and feasts. The same contents – '1 Table, 2 fformes, a gt cupboard, 1 little table' – listed in the 1705 inventory were still in place in 1874 with an additional table to store cutlery and a 'Japanned plate warmer'. Having lost its original furnishings, the room is today decorated faithfully with bucks' horns and in the service colours of brown and cream dating sometime before c.1940.

Above The Servants' Hall

Still Room (Kitchen)

The Still Room was the site of the original kitchen, placed within the house following the general practice of late 17th-century architects such as Roger Pratt. Around 1815 Sir Harry Fetherstonhaugh moved the kitchen to the East Service Block (today the café), again following contemporary opinion, to remove the source of smells and fire risk from the heart of the building.

The space was then probably used for multiple purposes, as the Still Room where cakes and preserves were made, tea and coffee prepared and a stopping place to make final touches to food before taking it to the Servery above. It also provided essential storage for crockery and served as a sitting room for the housekeeper and Still Room maids. Around 1895 the kitchen was brought back into this space and the 'New Gold Medal

Above The Kitchen, dominated by the large oak kitchen table

Eagle Range', supplied by the Eagle Range & Grate Co. of 127 Regent Street, London, was installed by Col Turnour-Fetherstonhaugh. It allowed for all forms of cooking: baking, roasting, boiling and keeping food warm. An 1874 inventory records '34 copper saucepans' in this room, and the large oak kitchen table and shelves now display a *batterie de cuisine* used in such a kitchen.

The Scullery was where the cutlery, crockery and glassware were washed; plates were dried in wooden racks above the sink. It was also used, in the 19th century, as a room for preparing pastry.

Butler's Pantry

The Butler's Pantry has been laid out to reflect past contents and, with the advice of professional butler Arthur Inch, to show how the space was used. The butler was the head of the team of male servants, responsible for waiting upon the heads of the family and their guests, for serving wine, food, tea and coffee, and laying the table in the Dining Room. This room provided the space needed to prepare for these duties and, being at the centre of the service areas, the ability to monitor comings and goings of staff and stock in the adjacent rooms.

In 1874, when Robert Friend was butler, the Pantry was used to store: glasses for water, champagne, claret, hock, sherry and liqueurs;

wine coolers, decanters, carafes and bottles; 'champagne nippers', a lever corkscrew, 14 brushes for silver plate and three clothes brushes; numerous candlesticks and snuffers; and 'about 16 lbs wax candles'. Almost all these items were valuable and so were stored either in locked cupboards or, as in the case of silver plate, in the safe. To maintain the accounts, the butler used a 'Mahogany Escritoire with bookcase top', he had a fire and 'foot warmer' and he, or the footman, could even sleep in the room on a 'Press bedstead' concealed in the cupboard.

The Lamp Room on the far right of the Butler's Pantry is a re-creation of the room used for preparing the lamps to light the house. In the late 19th century it contained 'Reading candles', 'Passage', 'Victor' and 'Argand' lamps as well as equipment for trimming wicks and filling oil.

Above The cast-iron range supplied by the Eagle Range & Grate Co. which manufactured products at its works in Catherine Street, Aston, Birmingham

Left The row of candle snuffers in the Lamp Room

Housekeeper's Room and Cellars

The housekeeper was the head female servant who looked after the household and cleaning, as well as attending to female family members and guests, and, at Uppark, was also responsible for the Still Room. Most is known about one particular housekeeper, Sarah Wells (1822–1905), due to the fact that her son, the writer H. G. Wells, wrote about her time here.

The house informed his novel *Tono-Bungay* in which he almost exactly describes this room:

'The much cupboarded, white-painted, chintz-brightened housekeeper's room where the upper servants assembled [and where] there was an old peerage and a Crockford … together with the books of recipes … on the little dresser that broke the cupboards on one side of my mother's room.'

The room was severely damaged by the fire with the floors above collapsing into it. Despite this, the cupboards and woodwork remained largely intact, and these and the walls have been repainted in the pre-Second World War colours of brown and cream. During restoration no fewer than 14 layers of off-white paint (as described by Wells) were discovered.

To the side is the housekeeper's closet in which were kept, according to the 1705 inventory, plates, tea and coffee pots, mugs, dessert glassware (such as 'Silleybub Glasses'), basins, a colander, wooden scales and weights, a coffee-mill and '13 Chamber pots'. Later inventories list the addition of preserves and pickle jars, as shown today, and ironing equipment.

Left The Housekeeper's Room where Sarah Wells must have pondered her unsuitability for the position, according to her son's disparaging account of her deficiencies

Bell Passage

In the 18th and 19th centuries this space was the domain of a bell-boy who waited to see which bell rang from the rooms above and alerted the relevant servants accordingly. From the second half of the 18th century elaborate bell systems were installed throughout the house. The larger of the two bell-boards was installed c.1800 with a pendulum below that continued to swing to give more notice to inattentive servants. In 1836 William Summers, a London 'Stove Manufacturer' and plumber, was recorded as 'Repairing and partly new hanging the Bells throughout the House'. The smaller board, and connecting wires to the larger bell-board, were installed between 1874 and 1893. It opened a named flap, obviating the need for a bell-boy.

Beer and Wine Cellars

The columns and vaulting of the Beer and Wine Cellars were installed when the house was built, in part to support the heavy marble floor once in the 'Greate hall' (now the Saloon) above. The exposed brick and basement level also provided the cooler temperatures required for storing alcohol. In 1706 there was both a 'Small beer Cellar' for lighter table ales (probably adjacent to the Steward's Hall) and a 'Strong beer Cellar' here, where no less than 1,900 gallons of ale were stored and beer pumped directly in from the brewhouse. By 1882 the Wine Cellar occupied the room off the main Beer Cellar, with brick bins to store brandies, gin, whisky, rum, sherry, burgundy, claret and champagne.

Above left **The Bell Passage with the door into the Beer Cellar on the left**

Above right **The Beer Cellar, housing the staple drink of the Servants' Hall until the 19th century. Small beer of low alcohol by volume was much safer to drink than water**

Steward's Hall and dolls' house

The original use of this room is not clear but its size suggests it was probably the Steward's Hall, as listed in 1704, where the senior servants would have dined. These included the butler, housekeeper, under-butler, housekeeper, valet, head housemaid and lady's maid.

Dolls' house

Today the Steward's Hall is home to a treasure of Uppark: one of the two most important 18th-century British dolls' houses. Made c.1735–40 for the Lethieuller family (their arms are painted onto the central pediment), the dolls' house was brought to Uppark by Sarah Lethieullier following her marriage to Sir Matthew Fetherstonhaugh in 1746.

The Uppark dolls' house is in remarkable condition, given its various historical locations (including different floors at Uppark) and was only slightly damaged when hurriedly evacuated during the fire. This dolls' house was an expensive status item rather than just a toy, intended for enjoyable, household-management instruction for women and perhaps for the children to play with, but only under supervision. H. G. Wells wrote in *Tono-Bungay* of playing 'discreetely' with the 'great dolls' house … under imperious supervision'.

The other important dolls' house of this type can be seen at Nostell Priory in West Yorkshire. Both are constructed as Palladian mansions, the balustrade surmounted with classical figures; they open from the front to give a snapshot of 18th-century life in a country house, accurate in every detail, from the individually oil-painted pictures to the real, hallmarked silver.

In its basement are the Kitchen, equipped with pewter plates, creamware pots and a cook in her printed cotton pinafore, the Staircase Hall furnished as an upper servants' dining room and the Housekeeper's Room with a toy tea-set, probably made in south Germany c.1725–50, and English glass of 1715–30.

On the ground floor are higher-ceilinged rooms, representing their higher status. In the Drawing Room the doll family sit around a silver table, surrounded by sumptuous furnishings

Below The Dining Room in the dolls' house. Its centrepiece is the blue japanned buffet with shelves for the display of silver and gold

such as a needlework carpet and landscape paintings. The Dining Room is placed centrally as was often the case in 17th- and 18th-century houses, with a blue japanned buffet with shelves to display silver and gold. The grandest bedrooms were situated on the ground floor until the end of the 18th century, and their beds are of a 'flying angel' type with the canopy supported on a hook in the ceiling. The lady of the house is 'lying in' after giving birth.

The grandest bedroom of the top floor is in the centre, with a gold silk bed flanked by four doors with pictures above. The blue-and-white porcelain in the rooms includes bottles made in Jingdezhen, China, c.1690–1725 and another made in Arita, Japan, c.1670–1700.

Above The Uppark dolls' house is remarkably similar to that at Nostell Priory, which is attributed to Thomas Chippendale

Service buildings

Opposite clockwise
from top left
The seven stalls for
horses in the West
Service Block.
A separate Harness
Room contained halters,
saddles and bridles

The East Service Block

The Game Larder,
from which flies were
excluded by finely
perforated metal sheets
over the windows

The subterranean
passage between the
house and service
blocks. The ladder
is a later addition

From the basement of the house, a network of tunnels leads to the service buildings. These were constructed c.1815 to connect the main elements of Repton's scheme, ensuring the hustle and bustle of service was kept from general view of the family and guests. They are lit and ventilated along the three main routes by ground-level apertures that can be seen around the turning circle and driveway.

East Service Block

Built, in part, to balance the stable block which was being constructed concurrently to the north west, the East Service Block was probably designed by James Paine or Daniel Garrett c.1750 – the bell in the tower above is dated 1754. The building was originally the 'Greenhouse and Laundry' and is still referred to as the 'Greenhouse Wing' in Repton's Red Book (see pages 54–5). The greenhouse occupied the south triple-height room with large windows, suitable for plants accustomed to warmer climates. In winter the greenhouse would have been further warmed by the stoves used in the Laundry behind. Around 1815 the kitchen was installed in the former greenhouse but moved back to the house around 1895. Its cast-iron range can still be seen in what is today the café.

Game Larder

Between the East Service Block and the driveway is a purpose-built larder for hanging game. It was probably designed by Repton, as it does not appear on his plan of the existing garden in 1810.

Meat would have been protected from flies by finely perforated sheet metal applied to the large windows which provided a necessary through draught. The first, octagonal room was designed for hanging bird carcasses and the second, rectangular room for venison.

West Service Block

The western service block was probably also designed by Paine or Garrett c.1750. The ground-floor space is configured with a '7 Stall Stable' and loose boxes, the finely carved acorn finials at the end of each bay indicating some status. The grooms lived in the attic spaces above the stable, to be on hand at all times to tend their charges. Adjacent buildings (now private) provided spaces for working horses, used on the farm and wider estate. Part of the space was converted in the 20th century to accommodate cars.

Dairy

The Dairy at Uppark is placed, rather strangely, facing south so taking the full heat of the sun, when dairy operations called for cold conditions. It was, however, conveniently located next to the farm and had a ready supply of ice from the two ice houses on the estate which facilitated the preparation of butter, cream and cheese. Built c.1800–15, the interior was renovated in 1832 with stained glass and ceramic tiles with a 'rich Enamelled Flower Border' supplied in 1832 by Charles Pepper, the London decorator. It is here that the then dairymaid, Mary Ann Bullock, worked and where Sir Harry overheard her singing one day, prompting his marriage proposal.

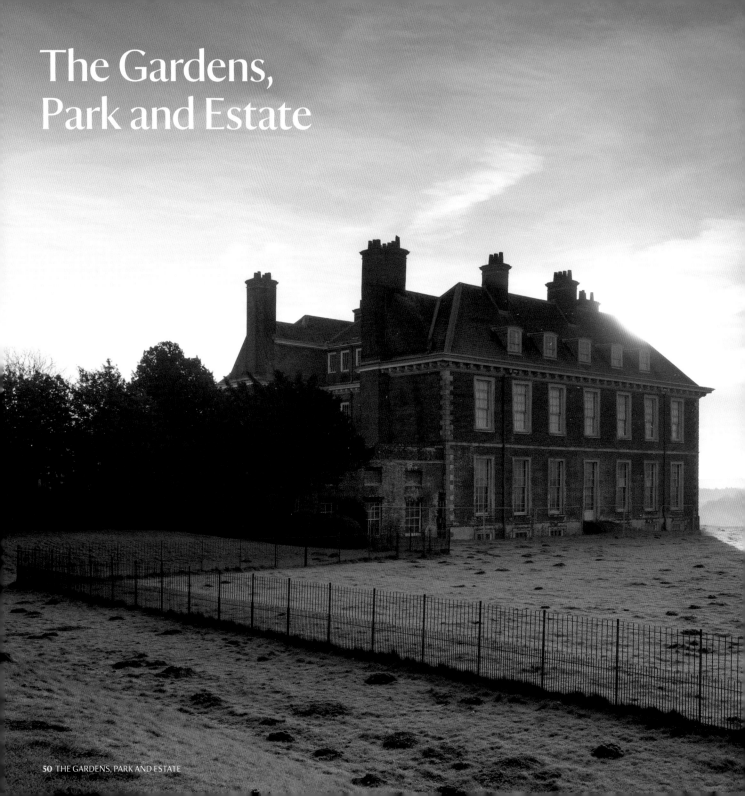

The Gardens,
Park and Estate

Left Uppark from the north-west

Gardens

Gardens have existed at Uppark since the 17th century. Today the gardens around the house are relatively young, having been largely recreated since storm damage in 1987.

The first account of the garden comes from 1695 when the traveller and writer Celia Fiennes visited, finding:

'fine gardens, gravell and grass walks and bowling green, with breast walls dividing each from the other … it looks very neate and all orchards and yards convenient.'

This description is supported by the Knyff engraving of c.1690. The fashionable formal gardens were possibly designed by the royal gardener George London who also worked at Hampton Court Palace and Petworth. The cost of a labour-intensive formal garden combined with the changing tastes of the next generation of Tankervilles probably encouraged its replacement by rolling terraces, apart from a small enclosure behind the house, by 1734, as Pieter Tillemans' painting shows.

When Sir Matthew bought Uppark in 1746, he ordered a survey and plan of his property from Thomas 'Sense' Browne and his assistant, James Crow. There is a record of Browne being paid £300 in March 1747 for his work. An unsigned plan, possibly the one commissioned, in the family archives, suggests garden features such as the rotunda and an area of open lawn surrounded by trees and shrubs. Confusion has led to the assumption that landscape designer Lancelot 'Capability' Brown was responsible for the plan, yet there are no references in 'Capability' Brown's account book or those of Sir Matthew to link him with Uppark. Entries in the account books for 1748 record gardening expenses which tally with the plan – 'To ye Menagerie for the Mans Wages 4.7.6' and to 'Francis Ruddall on acct., of Pond makg … 11.6.11'. Sir Matthew also planted orange and myrtle trees, at his wife's request, and kept a kitchen garden which had existed to the north east of the house since before 1746.

Alterations were made in the 19th century by Humphry Repton (see pages 54–5), pathway networks were in place by the mid-19th century and replanting continued throughout the 20th century – including a 'Sundial Bed' based on Repton's proposal, installed by Lady Meade-Fetherstonhaugh in 1933 (since removed), and further replanting following the Great Storm

of 1987. Today the gardens are presented in the picturesque Repton style, including a scented garden west of the drive to evoke the designer's belief in the importance of 'olfactory joy' in any garden. The main 'amphitheatre' garden, enclosed by knapped-flint walls, provides the required conditions for flowering shrubs, bulbs, perennials and herbaceous plants.

Opposite Mowing the east lawn with a horse c.1925

Below The mid-18th-century plan previously attributed to 'Capability' Brown

Head Gardener Billy Smith tending to the vines in the greenhouse c.1925

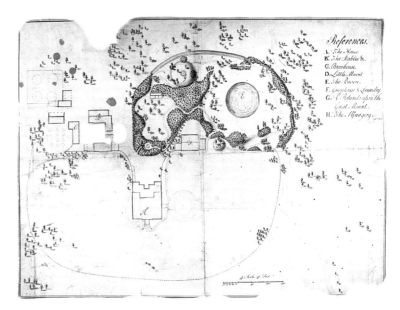

Repton at Uppark

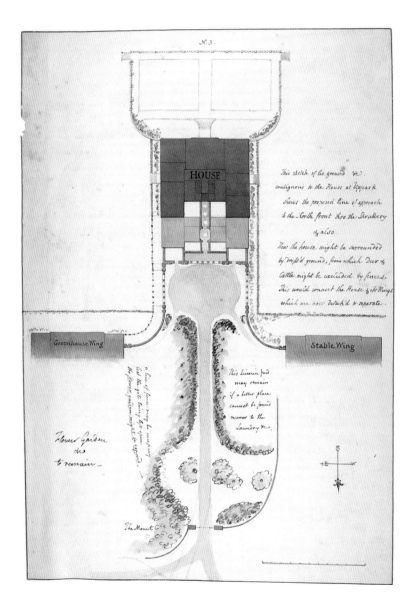

Left Repton's Red Book proposal for altering the approach to the north front

Born in Bury St Edmunds, Suffolk, Humphry Repton (1752–1818) spent his early years in East Anglia and the Netherlands, before returning to England to an apprenticeship as a textile merchant. This career seemed to hold little interest for Repton; in 1788 he decided to combine his artistic skills with his experience of arranging the grounds at his home in Sustead, Norfolk, to become a landscape gardener.

Repton sent out circulars to his friends and contacts, promoting his services and 'his skill in LANDSCAPE GARDENING'. The change of occupation proved a success and Repton designed more than 400 gardens during his 30-year career, including over 20 now cared for by the National Trust. Many of Repton's design proposals took the form of a leather-bound 'Red Book', so-called because of their scarlet bindings, with vibrant watercolour illustrations, costing about £42.

In 1810 Repton produced a 'Red Book' for Sir Harry Fetherstonhaugh, introduced with the line:

'It would appear presumptive of me to suggest any improvement or alteration to a place which possesses so many natural advantages as Uppark.'

Left An impression of the new approach to the north front, from Repton's Red Book for Uppark

Below An engraving of Humphry Repton after Samuel Shelley (1750/6–1808) who was a leading painter of portrait miniatures

Improvements and alterations were, nevertheless, suggested: the illustrations depict Uppark as Repton found it but an ingenious paper flap in the image could be pulled back to reveal his proposals beneath. His plans included a new landscaped driveway, flanked by beech trees (today acers), leading to a new porticoed entrance on the north side (added c.1811–14). Not all of his plans were realised: the carriage turning circle was intended to have a central lamppost and the house was to be linked by colonnades to the service blocks, but neither feature was installed.

Repton was probably responsible for two buildings in the garden, the Game Larder and the Dairy, and for placing a Coade stone copy of the Borghese Vase (the original is in the Louvre) on top of the mount in the Amphitheatre Garden. Sir Harry was certainly pleased with the work and asked Repton to make alterations to the house,

including the Servery, Dining Room, North Corridor and Saloon.

Correspondence between Repton and Sir Harry suggests the two struck up a friendship; their numerous letters to each other included comments on current affairs as well as aspects of their personal lives. In Repton's own words, Sir Harry became his 'bosom friend'.

A few years later, in 1817, with his health deteriorating, Repton wrote to Sir Harry asking for recommendations on reading matter and adding rather poignantly: 'I am tired of writing and my life you know was finished when I was last at Uppark.' Repton died the following year, aged 65, but two centuries later his work at Uppark lives on as the National Trust maintains and reinstates elements from his scheme.

Garden features

On entering Uppark through the 'golden gates', to the left lies a distinctive grassy mound dating from at least the 18th century which overlooks an open glade surrounded by shrubs and trees, within a walled garden.

This 'amphitheatre garden' is in the process of being replanted and landscaped to reflect the 19th-century pathways that weaved between trees and brought the owners and visitors of

Uppark to see the front of the house and views across the Downs. Maps of the 1870s show an extensive path network, confirmed by recent archaeology, but these were covered over in the 20th century. Over the next few years these paths will be reinstated to provide further access to the gardens as once intended, providing the key points from which visitors can get the best views of the gardens and landscape.

Above *View on the Downs near Uppark* by Pieter Tillemans (1684–1734), *c.*1728–30, showing the kitchen and stable blocks in their original positions when the drive led to the east front. To the south of the house is the short-lived circular pond

Around the south side of the mound is the Borghese Vase eye-catcher which Repton called 'The urn on the mount'. It is hidden by box and yew to allow for a delightful surprise as the sun catches the white Coade stone. Pioneered by the artist and businesswoman Eleanor Coade, the 'stone' material was made from a mix of clay, terracotta, silicates and glass fired for four days at extremely high temperatures. It was hard and fine enough to be moulded and carved with elaborate decoration, as in the Uppark example made *c.*1800.

Gothick Seat

Seating was always an important element of the garden with Sir Matthew Fetherstonhaugh's account book for 1758 recording 'Gothick seats at Uppark £70 19s 7d'. This particular Gothick Seat, overlooking the prime south-facing views, was almost certainly designed by Humphry Repton's antiquarian architect son, John Adey Repton, *c.*1811–14 and is very close in style to a seat commissioned for Sir Harry's friend, the Duke of Bedford, at Woburn, where Repton also worked.

Terraces

The south grass terraces running along the entire principal front of the house were the site of formal gardens to the west when the Tankerville house was first built. Pieter Tillemans' painting of 1728–30 shows the establishment of grass terraces, as today, rolling down to the former deer park and valley beyond. The painting also shows a large pond in front of the house, a short-lived feature though the outline can still be seen from above during dry weather. One of the glorious features of Uppark are the 'various views of Sea and Sand' from the terraces perched on the edge of the South Downs.

Above right **The Gothick seat to the north east of the house**

Right **The Coade stone two-thirds-size copy of the Borghese Vase, now in the Louvre**

Park and estate

Uppark's landscape setting has changed little over the centuries – woodlands to the north, open parkland to the south, giving way to the South Downs and the sea.

Le Uppeparke was stocked with deer from *c.*1332 and two-thirds of the land, cleared of trees, was given over to pasture for grazing animals. By 1440 both this and Le Netherpark (or Downpark) to the north were leased to Robert Legge, a London draper. 'Southdown' sheep fleeces were to become a profitable export as wool prices increased substantially in the

Below A shooting party at Uppark entering an old disused railway carriage for lunch, 1908

16th century and could be exported to Spain via nearby Portsmouth harbour only 18 miles away by horse and cart. The importance of timber for the estate was noted by Sir William Ford (b.1571) who complained to Parliament that the Puritans, in power, 'caused many of yr. Petitioner's trees to be cut downe close about his house which standeth upon a hill' no doubt for commercial gain.

In 1746 the timber in the park was substantial, being valued at the £19,000 paid by Sir Matthew Fetherstonhaugh for the whole estate. He went on to purchase other local estates and plant more chestnut and walnut trees. The park was stocked with red deer and pheasants, and even turtles were kept on the estate. In the wider estate to the north a fashionable tower 'folly' was completed in 1776, probably in celebration of Sir Harry's coming of age the year before. It was a site for food and entertainment, but was partly destroyed by fire in 1842.

After Sir Matthew's death in 1774, his wife Sarah managed the estate, paying for items such as:

'labour for mowing parks, and sundries £18.17.4' and '25 quarters of beans for deer £39.0.0'.

Sir Harry was not a natural countryman, despite commenting that 'there is no pursuit affording more rational amusement or more solid advantages than in the management of a farm'. Unlike the agricultural improvers of the age such as the nearby 3rd Earl of Egremont at Petworth, Sir Harry did, however, enjoy country sports such as 'hedge-row shooting in autumn'.

The estate was subsequently managed by his wife, Mary Ann, and her sister Frances, between them employing 203 workers across the 5,000-acre estate (including the 336-acre deer park) and handing on an 'intact and well maintained' estate to Col Turnour-Fetherstonhaugh in 1895. He continued the farming traditions at Uppark, breeding cows from the original Guernsey herd. By 1931, when the Meade-Fetherstonhaugh family came to Uppark, farming practice and technology had moved forward so the farm

horses, carts and traditional implements were sold. Today the Meade-Fetherstonhaugh family owns and manages the wider estate. Both they and the National Trust have undertaken extensive replanting of trees, particularly after major storms in the late 20th century. The National Trust looks after 21 hectares (52 acres) of land around Uppark house, including the garden, and a proportion of the Grade II-listed parkland and woodland.

Above *A View on the Downs near Uppark* by Pieter Tillemans (1684–1734), depicting the local Charlton hunt, probably painted in the 1720s

'colour and light shone in an unbroken tranquillity of peace, which impressed and held one.'

Margaret Meade-Fetherstonhaugh,
Uppark and its People (1964)

Conservation

Conservation of the structures at Uppark requires constant maintenance and often substantial investment. Despite the major conservation work after the fire in 1989, the subsequent years have taken their toll, particularly given Uppark's exposed position atop the South Downs which leads to substantial weathering and deterioration without constant care.

Inside the house, a deep clean by the house and collections team is undertaken each year to ensure the fragile collections and interiors are kept looking at their very best. Funded projects provide opportunities to focus on individual objects or aspects of the property, including the continued reinstatement of fire-damaged collections.

Above View from Uppark across the South Downs

Outside, the garden is assuming ever more of its picturesque Repton charm with the return of pathways to the formal gardens. For wildlife and nature conservation, the garden team sympathetically manages the gardens, grassland and woodland to encourage and conserve wildlife. Uppark provides a habitat for native brown hares in the grassland and woodland edges, helping to counter their population decline of 80 per cent during the last century because of modern agricultural practices and reduced habitat. Investing in the landscape will also benefit brown long-eared and common pipistrelle bats which are key species at Uppark, roosting in the roof of the house and spending their winter hibernation in the service tunnels.

Below A brown hare in the north drive with Repton's turning circle beyond, for which he intended a decorative eye-catcher

Uppark Today

Today Uppark is a tranquil and intimate property in a stunning location high on the South Downs with wonderful panoramic views to the sea.

The faded pink brickwork and the lichen-encrusted stone of the house settle it into the gentle landscape and prepare the visitor for the faded elegance of the interior. The house is famous as the 17th-century gem which was restored by the National Trust after the devastating fire of 1989, although the site has a much longer history which is inextricably interwoven to form the house and its setting as we see it today.

The resurrected skills and impressive crafts-manship that were deployed in the restoration of Uppark continue to inspire visitors, encouraging them to engage in conversation about the Trust's pioneering approach to caring for special places. Uppark is supported by a strong team of over 150 volunteers who work with National Trust staff to continue the tradition of careful conservation. Over the next few years a programme of major repairs and conservation work on the house and service buildings will continue. This work will be accompanied by the restoration of the historic path network around the gardens. Where once a relatively small number of private families and their staff experienced the 'peace and beauty' of the house and gardens, today the property attracts 80,000 visitors a year. Uppark is a place for everyone to enjoy.

Top row, left to right
The Staircase Hall with copy of the large parcel gilt side table destroyed in the fire

The French ormolu chandelier in the style of the *Régence* period (1715–23) in the Saloon

The north front

Bottom row, left to right
The west front from the Dairy

Detail of one of the scagliola table tops with landscape and flowers, made for Sir Matthew Fetherstonhaugh in 1754 by Pietro Belloni who lived in the monastery of Vallombrosa near Florence

The Saloon looking towards the Red Drawing Room; the pedestals are attributed to André-Charles Boulle

The family

As we look at the house today, thanks to the amazing restoration, it is hard to realise that the terrible tragedy of the fire ever struck Uppark in 1989.

Since completion of the restoration in 1995, our three families continue to enjoy Uppark and it is still very much our home. It is a wonderful house, which we all enjoy using for many family parties, weddings and christenings.

For all of us, the attraction of Uppark lies not only in the charming and beautiful house, but also its stunning setting. We take enormous pride in developing and maintaining the surrounding South Downs farmland which, we are proud to say now holds organic status.

Over the last few years, the arrival of 12 grandchildren, means the fifth generation is now able to enjoy the gardens and estate, hopefully with more to follow.

It is with much excitement that we look forward to adapting Uppark to the many and varied challenges of the 21st century. In doing so, we feel sure the house will always remain the centre of our family lives.

Harriet Cossart, Emma Goad and Sophie Warre

Below left Jean Meade-Fetherstonhaugh (1921–2006)

Below centre Richard Meade-Fetherstonhaugh (1913–58)

Below right Their grandchildren Charles, Maria, Edward, Oliver, Matilda, Harry and Theodora, sitting on the stairs in the Staircase Hall, c.1994